Dealing With Waste



# HOUSEHOLD WASTE

Sally Morgan

W
FRANKLIN WATTS
LONDON • SYDNEY

First published in 2006 by
Franklin Watts
338 Euston Road,
London NW1 3BH

Franklin Watts Australia
Hachette Children's Books
Level 17/207 Kent Street,
Sydney NSW 2000



Produced for Franklin Watts by White-Thomson Publishing Ltd
210 High Street,
Lewes BN7 2NH

Editor: Rachel Minay
Designer: Brenda Cole
Picture research: Morgan Interactive Ltd
Consultant: Graham Williams

Picture credits:
The publishers would like to thank the following for reproducing these photographs:
Digitalvision front cover main image & top right; Ecoscene front cover bottom right (Angela Hampton), 6 (Jon Bower), 7 (Rod Gill), 8 (Alan Towse), 9 (Sally Morgan), 10 (Tom Ennis), 11 (Luc Hosten), 12 (Nick Hawkes), 13 (Vicki Coombs), 14 (Adrian Morgan), 15 (Lorenzo Lees), 16 (Vicki Coombs), 17 (Angela Hampton), 18 (Alan Towse), 19 (Nick Hanna), 21 (Phillip Colla), 22 (Vicki Coombs), 23 (Wayne Lawler), 24 (Martin Jones), 25 (Latha Raman), 26 (Peter Landon), 27 (Angela Hampton).



British Library Cataloguing in Publication Data
A CIP catalogue record for this book
is available from the British Library.

ISBN-10: 0 7496 6432 0
ISBN-13: 978 0 7496 6432 9

Dewey classification: 363.72'88

Printed in China

# Contents

# Mountains of waste

**Every day we throw away mountains of waste. This includes packaging from food and goods, paper and envelopes, cans and bottles, plastic bags, kitchen waste and much more.**

Shoppers crowd this street in Shenyang in China. As the standard of living increases in countries such as China, the waste problem will grow.

## More people, more waste

As the number of people in the world increases so does the amount of waste. However, not all parts of the world produce the same amount of waste. A typical home in a developed country such as the USA, UK or Germany produces many times more waste than a home in a developing country such as Kenya, Ghana or India. For example, on average a person in the USA produces about 2 kg of waste per day, a person in Europe produces about 1.1 kg per day while a person living in India produces just over 0.5 kg of waste per day.

## Thrown away

As people earn more money, they buy more goods, especially electrical goods and luxury items. They throw away more, too. The world is changing from one where people used to repair broken goods or reuse them to one in which broken objects are tossed away and replaced by new ones. The manufacture of all these goods is using up the world's resources.

In some places waste is dumped on the side of the road, creating an unsightly mess and attracting pests such as rats and mice.

## It's my world!

**How much waste does your family produce each day? Put one day's waste into a bag and weigh it. Can you work out how much your family would throw away in a year?**

### Harming the environment

Waste can be very harmful to the environment if it is not disposed of carefully. Also, the increasing volumes of waste create problems for the people who have to dispose of it. The world cannot continue to create so much waste – everybody will have to find ways of reducing it.

In this book you will read about the different types of waste that people produce and how we deal with it.

# What's in your rubbish?

**People throw away all sorts of things. Much of the waste comes from the kitchen or garden. There are food scraps, lawn clippings and weeds as well as paper, plastic and metals.**

## Biodegradable waste

Food and garden waste is described as being biodegradable. This means that it will rot or break down naturally. The first stages of this rotting process often take place in the bin when food goes mouldy and becomes smelly! Some people put a lot of garden waste in their bins. This type of waste should be put on a compost heap where micro-organisms such as bacteria and fungi break it down.

Compost needs a good mix of materials such as food scraps and grass clippings to make sure it does not turn into a sloppy mess. Shredded paper and cardboard can also be composted.

## It's my world!

**Not everybody has a compost bin. However, many towns and cities have facilities where people can take their garden waste. The waste is put on large compost heaps where it breaks down to form compost, which people can buy to put on their gardens. Find out where your local compost facilities are located. This information can often be found on the Internet.**

## Other waste

A lot of paper is thrown away, too. This includes newspapers, magazines, old envelopes, junk mail, waste bits of paper and cardboard boxes. There is paper packaging from around food and household goods. The rest of the waste is made up of plastic, metals and glass, together with old clothes, unwanted toys, other household items and things that have been broken beyond repair.

Much of this rubbish bin could have been recycled, including all of the glass and metal and most of the plastic and paper. All the kitchen and garden waste could have been composted. That adds up to about 80% of the waste.

## Dangerous waste

Some of the things that we throw away can harm the environment. For example, old batteries contain metals that are poisonous to wildlife. Sometimes people throw away unused medicines, which should be returned to the chemist to be disposed of properly. Many chemicals are used in the garden, which should not be put in the rubbish but disposed of carefully.

# Where does your waste go?

**What happens to the waste you throw out? In most developed countries, the waste is collected and taken to either landfill sites or incinerators. However, in much of the developing world, rubbish is just dumped in the countryside.**

## Landfills

Landfills are huge holes in the ground, often left by gravel pits and quarries. The hole is gradually filled with waste from homes and industry. Each day, tractors squash the waste down so that it is all compacted together with no holes. Once the hole is full the top is covered with a layer of soil. After about ten years the land can be used for farming, as a park or for playing fields.

Dumping waste in a hole is easy, but landfills cause problems. People don't like living near them as the waste attracts pests such as rats and seagulls. Landfills can be smelly places. As all the food and garden waste rots down, it releases a gas called methane. This gas has to be piped away – otherwise it could cause an explosion. Also, there are only a limited number of landfills and they are rapidly filling up.

This digger is flattening the waste that has been tipped in a landfill so that it does not fill up so much space. The food in the waste attracts flocks of gulls.

# It's my world!

Never litter the environment as it could harm animals. Animals may crawl into bottles and cans looking for food and become trapped. Birds may become entangled in plastic netting or get their necks trapped in plastic rings. Broken glass on the ground could cut the feet of people as well as animals.

## Incinerators

Incinerators are places where waste is burnt. Some modern incinerators use the heat produced by the burning waste to generate electricity. These incinerators are called waste-to-energy plants.

There are problems with incinerators, too. The smoke from incinerators may contain dangerous chemicals such as dioxin. Tiny quantities of this chemical causes ill health and can even kill people.

## Better to recycle

Much of the waste that ends up in landfills and incinerators could be recycled. If it is recycled, it can be used to make something else. This is much better for the environment.

This gannet on a beach in South Africa has become entangled in a sheet of plastic. Many animals die each year after becoming tangled in plastic rubbish.

# Reduce, reuse and recycle

The three 'R's of managing waste are 'reduce', 'reuse' and 'recycle'. Reduce means to cut down on the amount of waste, reuse means to put something to a new use or to mend it rather than throw it away and recycle means to make a material into a new product.

Fruit and vegetables in a market are sold without unnecessary packaging. In the supermarket, you can choose loose rather than pre-packaged produce.

## Reduce and reuse

It is much better not to produce any waste in the first place. If less waste is thrown away, there is less waste to bury in landfills or burn in incinerators. For example, disposable nappies are a substantial part of household waste in houses where there is a baby. This could be avoided by using washable nappies. The next best way to deal with waste is to reuse it. For example, old plastic pots can be used as plant pots. Another way of reusing something is to sell it or give it to a charity shop or jumble sale. If something cannot be reused then the next best thing is to recycle it.

## It's my world!

Try to reduce the amount of packaging in your waste. Always take a shopping bag with you so you don't have to pick up lots of new plastic bags. Try to choose goods with fewer layers of unnecessary packaging. Once you have removed all the packaging, make sure you recycle as much of it as possible.

## Recycle

Recycling means to make something into a new item – for example a glass bottle can be melted down and made into a new bottle while old cardboard can be shredded and made into new cardboard. Virtually all the world's countries have recycling schemes. A wide range of items can be recycled but the most common are glass, paper, metal, plastic, old clothes, oil and batteries. There are recycling facilities such as bottle banks near shops and car parks and items for recycling are often collected from the home.

So remember the three Rs – reduce, reuse and recycle. It is always better to reduce first, then reuse something and lastly recycle something.

Car boot or yard sales are good places to sell unwanted toys, books, clothes and other household goods.

# Dealing with glass

**Glass is a very useful material. It can be made into bottles, jam jars and other containers to hold liquids and foods. Also, it can be recycled over and over again.**

## Reusing glass bottles

It is much better for the environment to reuse a glass bottle than to recycle it. Glass bottles can be collected, washed and refilled. Bottles that are reused have to be a bit heavier than other bottles so they do not break or chip easily. In Europe, bottles used for milk or beer may be reused more than 30 times and have a life of four years. In the developing world it is common for glass bottles to be collected and reused.

These glass bottles outside a shop in Jakarta, Indonesia, are awaiting collection. They will be taken to the local factory, cleaned and refilled.

## Recycling glass bottles

Bottles for recycling are collected at bottle banks. The glass is crushed to form cullet, which is transported to glass factories.

Glass is made from sand, soda ash and limestone. Additives may be used to give the glass a colour or to make it more resistant to heat. These raw materials are heated in a furnace to 1,800 °C so they melt. The molten glass is poured into moulds to form new bottles. Cullet is usually added to the furnace with the raw materials, so fewer raw materials are required to make the glass.

Clear glass is the most valuable as it has many uses. A lot of brown glass is used for beer bottles. Green glass is the least useful and is used mostly for wine bottles. Glass can be also recycled into a road surface called glasphalt, garden paving and decorative jewellery.

The different coloured glass has to be kept separate, so there are normally three bottle banks, one each for clear, green and brown glass.

**Make sure that every glass bottle and container used by your family is recycled. There are plenty of glass-recycling banks. You usually find them in the car park of a supermarket or shopping centre. Local authorities have recycling facilities that will have glass banks. In some places glass is collected from homes.**

## Benefits of recycling

Recycling glass saves energy as glass made with cullet melts at a lower temperature than glass made from raw materials, so less energy is used to heat the materials in the furnace. It reduces the air pollution produced by glass manufacturing by 20% and the water pollution by 50%. It means less glass ends up in landfills and less broken glass is lying around to harm people and wildlife.

# Paper and cardboard

**Paper is an incredibly useful material that is used in newspapers, magazines and books. One of its most common uses is in packaging for food and other goods. Paper, such as newspaper, is already made from recycled paper. Most other paper can also be recycled after use.**

This waste paper has been sorted and baled. Recycling paper reduces the amount of waste that ends up in landfill sites.

## From paper bank to paper mill

Paper for recycling has to be sorted, graded and baled before it can be transported to a paper mill. In the paper mill the recycled paper is broken up into a pulp. It is then mixed with lots of water and chemicals to make a mush that is used to form paper. Sometimes, some unrecycled pulp is added to improve the quality of the final paper. The runny mush is spread out over a moving belt of the paper machine and the water drains away. The paper is now a continuous layer and is passed through a series of heated rollers so that it is flattened, dried and ironed to give it a polished surface. Finally the paper is rolled onto huge reels and taken to the cutting room to be cut into sheets.

## Fibres

If you look at paper under a microscope you will see that it is made from lots of fibres squashed together. The longer the fibre is, the better quality the paper. However, each time paper is recycled the fibres get shorter. Shorter lengths of fibre make poorer quality paper such as newspaper print. One of the biggest users of recycled paper is the newspaper industry. Other poor quality paper is recycled to make cardboard and toilet paper.

When you buy stationery in the shops check the packaging to see if it has been made from recycled paper.

## It's my world!

There are lots of ways of reducing your use of paper.

- Scraps of paper can be made into notebooks.
- Only throw away a sheet of paper once it has been written on both sides.
- Don't print out unnecessary pages on your printer – look at them on the screen instead.
- E-mails are quicker and cheaper to send than a letter and they don't use any paper or envelopes.
- Reuse envelopes by sticking a label over the old address.

## Other uses of paper

Not all paper is recycled back to paper. Nowadays it is possible to buy animal bedding that is made from recycled paper. Paper can also be made into a 'fluff' that is used to insulate homes. The fluff is pumped into the gap between the inner and outer wall of bricks to prevent heat from escaping. Some recycled paper is used to make disposable nappies.

# Metals for recycling

**Metals are valuable materials as they can be used in many ways. A variety of metals can be found in the home, for example steel and aluminium in cans and aerosols, lead on the roof, copper piping, and gold and silver in jewellery.**

Metal cans are moved along a conveyor belt in a large recycling centre in Florida. They will be crushed and baled and sent to a factory where they will be melted down.

## Where metal comes from

Most metals cannot be dug straight from the ground. A metal usually occurs as an ore, for example iron is found in iron ore and aluminium occurs as an ore called bauxite. The ores are found in rocks so they have to be quarried or mined from the ground. Then the ores have to be crushed and transported to factories where they are heated to high temperatures to extract the metal.

## Easy to recycle

Recycling metal is much easier compared with extracting the metal from rocks. Metals are very easy to recycle and they can be recycled over and over again. Waste metal is tipped into a large furnace and heated to a high temperature so that it melts. The molten metal is poured into a mould to make an ingot. The ingots are stored until the metal is needed to make something. Then it is melted again and reshaped into a new object.

## Helping the environment

Recycling metal helps the environment. A lot of fuel is used to dig the rocks from the ground and then transport them around the world. More fuel is needed to extract the metal from the rock. In comparison, melting down old metal takes much less energy. The extraction process creates air and water pollution, too. Mining and quarrying damages habitats. Often quarries are located in attractive parts of the countryside and they create unsightly scars. Recycling metal takes place locally, so the metal does not have to be transported far.

## Did you know...?

Steel and aluminium cans look very similar. One way to tell them apart is to use a magnet. Steel is magnetic, so a steel can will stick to a magnet. Aluminium is not magnetic, so a magnet will not pick up an aluminium can. It is important to be able to tell the difference as the two metals have to be kept separate when they are recycled.Test some cans yourself to see if they are magnetic or not. You may need to check the top and the sides of the can as sometimes the sides and ends are made from different metals.

Quarries, such as this bauxite quarry in Jamaica, destroy habitats and create piles of waste. The quarried rock is crushed and shipped overseas.

# Recycling plastics

**Plastics are useful materials. Each year, 100 million tonnes of plastics are made around the world. That uses up a lot of oil.**

### What is plastic?

Most plastics are made from oil. Plastics are made up of long chains of molecules and these chains are formed when oil is heated. There are more than 50 different groups of plastic. Hard plastics are used to make containers and bottles. Thin and flexible plastics are used to make plastic bags. Foam-like plastics are used in disposable plastic cups and takeaway packaging. All these different plastics have to be kept separate when they are recycled.

## Identifying plastics

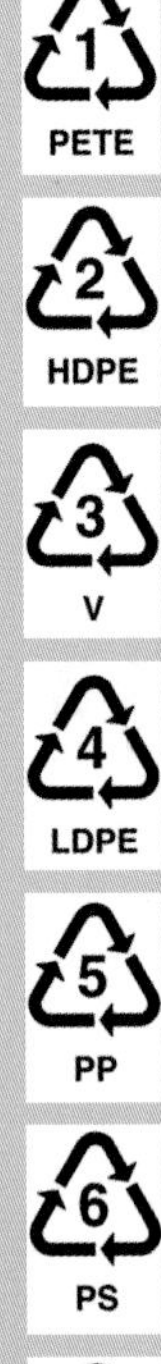

| Symbol | Plastic | Uses |
|---|---|---|
|  1 PETE | Polyethylene terephthalate | Fizzy drink bottles and oven-ready meal trays |
|  2 HDPE | High-density polyethylene | Bottles for milk and washing-up liquids |
| 3 V | Polyvinyl chloride | Food trays, cling film, bottles for squash, mineral water and shampoo bottles |
| 4 LDPE | Low density polyethylene | Carrier bags and bin liners |
| 5 PP | Polypropylene | Margarine tubs, microwaveable meal trays |
|  6 PS | Polystyrene | Yoghurt pots, foam food trays, hamburger boxes and egg cartons, vending cups, plastic cutlery |
| 7 OTHER | | Any other plastics that do not fall into any of the above categories, for example melamine, which is used in plastic plates and cups |

## Sorting plastic

It is possible to recycle almost all types of plastic, but only a few types are recycled at the moment. This is because some plastics, such as blended plastics (which are made from several types of plastic), are very difficult to recycle. Recycling certain plastics can damage the environment because they release harmful chemicals during the recycling process, so it is better not to recycle them. Plastic bottles are the most useful, while plastic food wrappers and yoghurt pots are not widely recycled. To make it easier for the public and people sorting plastics at recycling centres, most plastic items carry a logo (see table), which identifies the type of plastic they are made from. The logo is a recycling triangle with a number in the middle – the number identifies the plastic.

**How many plastic bags did you pick up from shops this week? Try to reduce the number of plastic bags you use by having strong reusable bags for your shopping. You can use plastic bags to line waste bins. Plastic containers can be useful, too. Try using them as plant pots or as containers for small objects such as buttons, nails and screws. Attractive pots can be used on a desk for paper clips and pens.**

## Processing plastic

Before plastic waste can be recycled it has to be separated into different types and colours. Then it is cleaned, shredded into small flakes and bagged. The flakes are transported to factories where they are heated so that they melt and are shaped into new objects. A wide range of items can be made from recycled plastic, for example, bin liners, plant pots, drain pipes, animal feed troughs, window frames, water butts, fencing and garden benches and chairs. Plastic bottles are even made into fleece clothes.

These tourists watching the Old Faithful Geyser in Yellowstone National Park in the USA are standing on a viewing platform made from recycled plastic.

# Dangerous waste

**People throw all sorts of things into the bin without thinking about whether they are safe. A number of dangerous chemicals are used in the home and if they get into the environment they can harm wildlife.**

### Chemicals in the garden shed

Many harmful chemicals may be found in the garden shed or garage. These could include pesticides, weedkillers and slug pellets. There may be pots of old paint, paint stripper or antifreeze. All of these chemicals could harm the environment if they were tipped down the drain, if they leaked out of the bin or were dumped in a landfill.

### Chemicals for cleaning

The cupboard under the kitchen sink is often packed with cleaning materials such as bleach and other chemicals. Some are so powerful that the person using them must wear protective gloves. The contents should never be tipped down the sink or put in the bin without being securely wrapped to prevent leaks.

Paint contains harmful chemicals. Leftover paint should never be tipped down the drain or sink. There is usually somewhere in your local area where paint can be disposed of safely.

### Harmful batteries

Batteries contain metals such as mercury, nickel and cadmium, all of which are very harmful. Single-use batteries (also called alkaline batteries) are thrown away once they are flat. They contain metals such as mercury, silver or zinc. Rechargeable batteries or NiCads contain the metals nickel and cadmium, which are also hazardous. Lithium ion batteries are used in laptops but they are not considered to be dangerous. The amount of harmful metal in batteries, especially mercury, has been declining in recent years and now it is possible to buy mercury-free batteries. Often there are collection points for old batteries in shops and at recycling centres.

When chemical containers, even empty ones, are dumped into landfill sites, there is a possibility that any liquid in the container will drain out into the soil.

## Did you know...?

**There are many potentially harmful chemicals in the home. Some of the most common ones are:**

- bleach
- oven cleaner
- solvents in glue and cleaning agents
- white spirit
- paint stripper (turpentine)
- pesticide
- weedkiller
- slug pellets
- batteries
- antifreeze
- unwanted or outdated medicines
- fluorescent light bulbs.

## It's my world!

**The chemicals mentioned on this page have to be disposed of carefully so that they do not harm the environment. Local authorities usually have websites telling you where to take different chemicals and how to wrap them up.**

# The developing world

**There is far less waste in the developing world. People cannot afford to throw things away and so there is far more reuse and recycling of unwanted items.**

These oilcans have been made from old beer cans.

## Waste scavengers

There are huge waste dumps in some of the cities of the developing world, such as Mexico City in Mexico and Manila in the Philippines. Here, people spend the day searching through the waste looking for useful items. These people are called waste scavengers and they earn their living by collecting and selling waste. Often they are women and children and they work with little protection for their hands and feet. However, waste scavengers have an important role to play. They make sure that all the recyclable materials are removed and recycled. This reduces the amount of waste that is in the dump.

## Making new from old

Many things are never thrown away but reused to make new items, for example rubber soles are removed from old shoes and stuck onto new ones while aluminium cans are used as building materials. Toys can be made from old wheels and bits of wire. By being imaginative, people can made a whole range of essential items from waste.

**Imagine you had to find a present for a friend but you didn't have any money. Could you make something from recycled items such as old wheels, metal coat hangers, string, pieces of wood and plastic?**

## Plastic rubbish

Lots of plastic bags are used around the world. Unfortunately, in some developing countries rubbish is left on the streets and the plastic bags blow away in the wind and litter the streets. Plastic litter is a big problem in some countries such as The Gambia. The bags get caught on fences and trees or end up in rivers. Sometimes animals get caught up in the plastic bags and they can die. Countries such as South Africa and Bangladesh are now banning the manufacture of plastic bags.

## Did you know...?

**India recycles about 60% of the plastic used each year, a figure higher than any other country. The average for the rest of the world is about 20%. India is able to achieve such a high rate because wages are low and recycling companies can afford to employ the many people needed to sort through all the plastic waste. In the UK, more than 80% of plastic waste from households ends up in landfills and only about 7% is recycled. The rest is burnt.**

These Indian workers are sorting different types of plastic. The plastic could cut their skin or be covered in harmful substances, but they do not wear any protective clothing or gloves on their hands.

# The way ahead

**The amount of waste that is being produced by people is increasing every year. Landfill sites are filling up and it has become more expensive to dispose of all the waste. Somehow more waste will have to be recycled.**

Goods such as Easter eggs and boxes of chocolates come with layers of unnecessary packaging.

## Encouraging recycling

One way to encourage people to throw away less is to charge them for every kilogram of waste they put out for collection. This is called 'Pay-As-You-Throw' in the USA and these schemes have resulted in a sharp decrease in the amount of waste. Often people are more likely to recycle if the items are collected from their own homes rather than if they have to drive to a recycling point.

## Passing laws

Governments can encourage more recycling by making manufacturers responsible for disposing of items such as packaging. Laws can be passed that require manufacturers to use a certain percentage of recycled materials in their manufacturing processes.

If your home does not have a recycling collection simply place all the bottles and other items that can be recycled in a box and when you go shopping with your family they can be emptied into recycling bins.

## Creating a demand

Recycling schemes need a market for recycled materials. There is no point collecting glass or plastic for recycling if nobody wants to buy it. So it is important that people buy items containing recycled materials. This will create a demand for the recycled materials and they will become more valuable. When a recycled material is valuable, for example metal, people are more likely to want to recycle it.

When you buy stationery, such as notepads or envelopes, check to see if it is made from recycled paper. If it is, it will have a recycling logo with a percentage in the middle. This tells you exactly how much recycled paper was used in its manufacture.

## It's my world!

There are many ways to reduce the amount of waste you and your family throw away each week. See if you can cut down on your waste. Some ways are very simple. For example, recycle as much as possible and don't put glass, paper, plastic or metal in the bin. See what else you could recycle, for example batteries and old clothes. If you have a garden, put food scraps on a compost heap or see if your local council runs a food composting scheme.

# Glossary

**Biodegradable**
able to be broken down naturally by micro-organisms such as bacteria and fungi

**Compost**
to break down waste garden matter. Compost is a soil-like material that is full of nutrients

**Cullet**
broken or waste glass to be recycled

**Developed country**
a country in which most people have a high standard of living

**Developing country**
a country in which most people have a low standard of living and who have poor access to goods and services compared with people in a developed country

**Incinerator**
a place where waste is burnt

**Ingot**
a block of metal such as gold, silver or steel

**Landfill**
a large hole in the ground that is used to dispose of waste

**Ore**
a type of rock that contains metal in sufficient quantity to be mined

**Pollution**
the release of harmful substances into the environment

**Recycle**
to process and reuse materials in order to make new items

**Reduce**
to lower the amount of waste that is produced

**Reuse**
to use something again, either in the same way or in a different way

**Waste**
anything that is thrown away, abandoned, or released into the environment in a way that could harm the environment

# Websites

**British Glass Recycling**
www.recyclingglass.co.uk
Website about recycling glass in the UK, aimed primarily at young people.

**Can Smart**
www.cansmart.org
Australian website dealing with the recycling of steel cans.

**Freecycle**
www.freecycle.com
Website where members can send e-mails to other members of the group listing items that they want to recycle free of charge rather than dumping them on a landfill site.

**Friends of the Earth**
www.foe.org.uk
Website of the charity Friends of the Earth. It gives information about current campaigns – including those for encouraging recycling and against incinerators and landfills.

**Let's Recycle**
www.letsrecycle.com/index.jsp
Website looking at all sorts of waste and how it can be recycled.

**Ollie Recycles**
www.ollierecycles.com/recycle/index.html
Website with information on recycling in the UK and Australia, aimed at young people.

**Recycle Now**
www.recyclenow.com/index.html
Really useful UK website covering recycling at home, in the garden, at work, at school, at the shops and at leisure.

**United States Environmental Protection Agency**
www.epa.gov
This website has lots of environmental information on all issues, not just waste. There is an EPA Kids Club (www.epa.gov/kids) with information on waste and recycling.

**Waste Online**
www.wasteonline.org.uk
Comprehensive website looking at all aspects of recycling.

**World Aluminium Institute**
www.world-aluminium.org
Website with details about aluminium, where it is found, how it is extracted and then recycled.

Every effort has been made by the Publisher to ensure that these websites are suitable for children and contain no inappropriate or offensive material. However, because of the nature of the internet it is impossible to guarantee that the contents of these sites will not be altered. We strongly advise that internet access is supervised by a responsible adult.

# Index

AFRICA FOCUS

# ANCIENT AFRICA

Rob Bowden and Rosie Wilson

**www.heinemannlibrary.co.uk**
Visit our website to find out more information about Heinemann Library books.

**To order:**
Phone +44 (0) 1865 888066
Fax +44 (0) 1865 314091
Visit www.heinemannlibrary.co.uk


First published in hardback in 2009



Edited by Louise Galpine and Rachel Howells
Designed by Richard Parker and Manhattan Design
Original illustrations © Capstone Global Library Ltd
Illustrated by Oxford Designers and Illustrators
Picture research by Mica Brancic
Originated by Heinemann Library
Printed in China by Leo Paper Products Ltd.

ISBN 9780 431 02075 4 (hardback)
13 12 11 10 09
10 9 8 7 6 5 4 3 2 1

**British Library Cataloguing in Publication Data**
Bowden, Rob
Ancient Africa. - (Africa focus)
I. Title II. Wilson, Rosalind
960.1

A full catalogue record for this book is available from the British Library.

**Acknowledgements**

We would like to thank the following for permission to reproduce photographs: akg-images p. **40**; Corbis pp. **10 & 14** (© The Gallery Collection), **13** (Robert Harding World Imagery/1996-98/AccuSoft Inc., All Rights), **23** (© Tim Graham), **26** (Werner Forman), **27** (Sergio Pitamitz/zefa), **35** (Bojan Brecelj), **39** (© Corbis); EASI-Images pp. **25 & 29** (Roy Maconachie); Getty Images pp. **5** (Hulton Archive/Stringer), **7** (Melville B. Grosvenor/National Geographic), **15** (Robert Harding World Imagery/Andrew McConnell), **31** (Photographer's Choice/Sylvain Grandadam), **32** (Time Life Pictures/Mansell/Time Life Pictures), **33** (Henry Guttmann/Stringer/Hulton Archive), **41** (Hulton Archive/Stringer Collection); Library of Congress p. **38**; Lonely Planet Images p. **20** (Ariadne Van Zandbergen); Photolibrary pp. **4** (Phototake Science/Carolina Biological Supply Company), **8** (John Warburton-Lee Photography/Susanna Wyatt), **9** (Oxford Scientific/Ariadne Van Zandbergen), **18** (JTB Photo), **30** (John Warburton-Lee Photography/Nigel Pavitt); The Bridgeman Art Library p. **37**.

Cover photograph of bronze head, Benin, reproduced with permission of Corbis (Christie's Images).

We would like to thank Danny Block for his invaluable help in the preparation of this book.

# Contents



Some words are printed in bold, **like this**. You can find out what they mean by looking in the glossary on page 44.

# An ancient land

The study of ancient humans looks at how people lived in the distant past. Our human **ancestors** were living in Africa over 1.6 million years ago! In fact, scientists believe that human life began in Africa and so the ancient history of Africa is in some ways the ancient history of us all. These first ancestors lived **primitive** lives, but Africa also holds the secrets of early societies that were rich and highly organized. We know this because of treasures and objects that were left behind. **Fossils**, bones, tools, and art have been found across the **continent**.

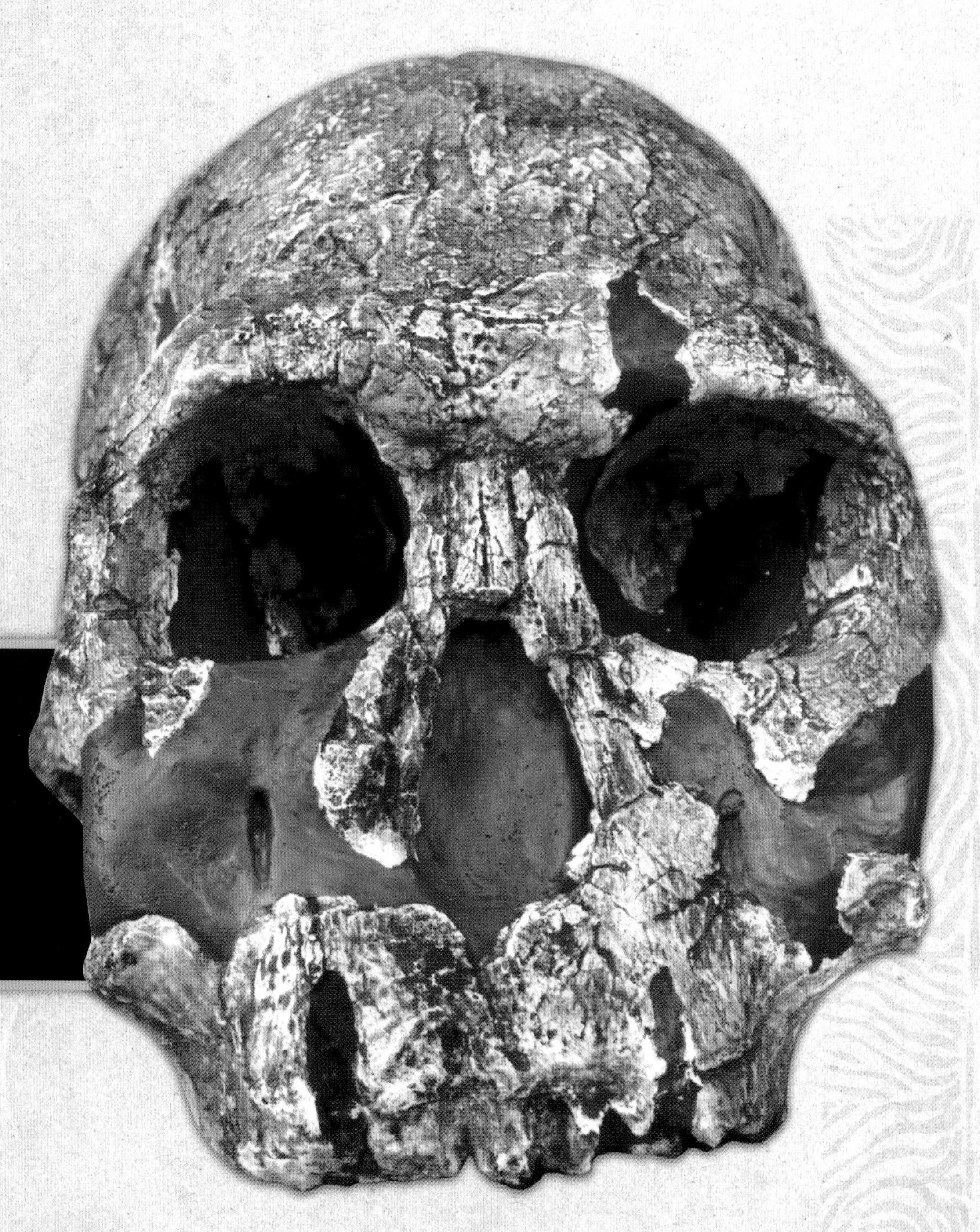

This ancient human skull was found at Koobi Fora, Kenya, in 1972. It is thought to be around 1.9 million years old.

This group of African slaves is in Tanzania in 1896. They are wearing chains and being guarded by a soldier.

## Great societies

Africa has seen the rise and fall of many great societies. They grew strong by using or trading the continent's rich **resources**. These included gold, salt, **ivory**, and people who were traded as **slaves**. Many of the earliest crafts and skills, including farming, carpentry, and metalwork, were developed by these societies. They may be long gone now, but in parts of Africa you can still see evidence of how these societies might have lived.

## Africa and the world

It was only about 500 years ago that explorers and traders from Europe and America began to reveal Africa's secrets to the rest of the world. They returned with stories of rich resources and great opportunities for **trade**. Powerful European countries sent explorers and armies to take advantage of this. They brought back gold, spices, and other fascinating items. They also took people as slaves and shipped them to work in the Americas. Millions of people were taken as slaves and African societies suffered greatly. Slavery eventually ended in the 19th century, but by then Africa had been weakened and had fallen to the control of European countries.

# The origin of humankind

All living things on Earth are given a scientific name. This allows us to see how different **species** are related and how they develop over time. Modern humans, like you and I, are known scientifically as *Homo sapiens sapiens*. Modern humans first appeared around 170,000 years ago in eastern or southern Africa. Earlier human **ancestors** had already been living in Africa as well as in Europe and Asia, but *Homo sapiens sapiens* gradually replaced them. They spread from Africa across Asia and Europe, and eventually reached the Americas, Australia, and even remote islands.

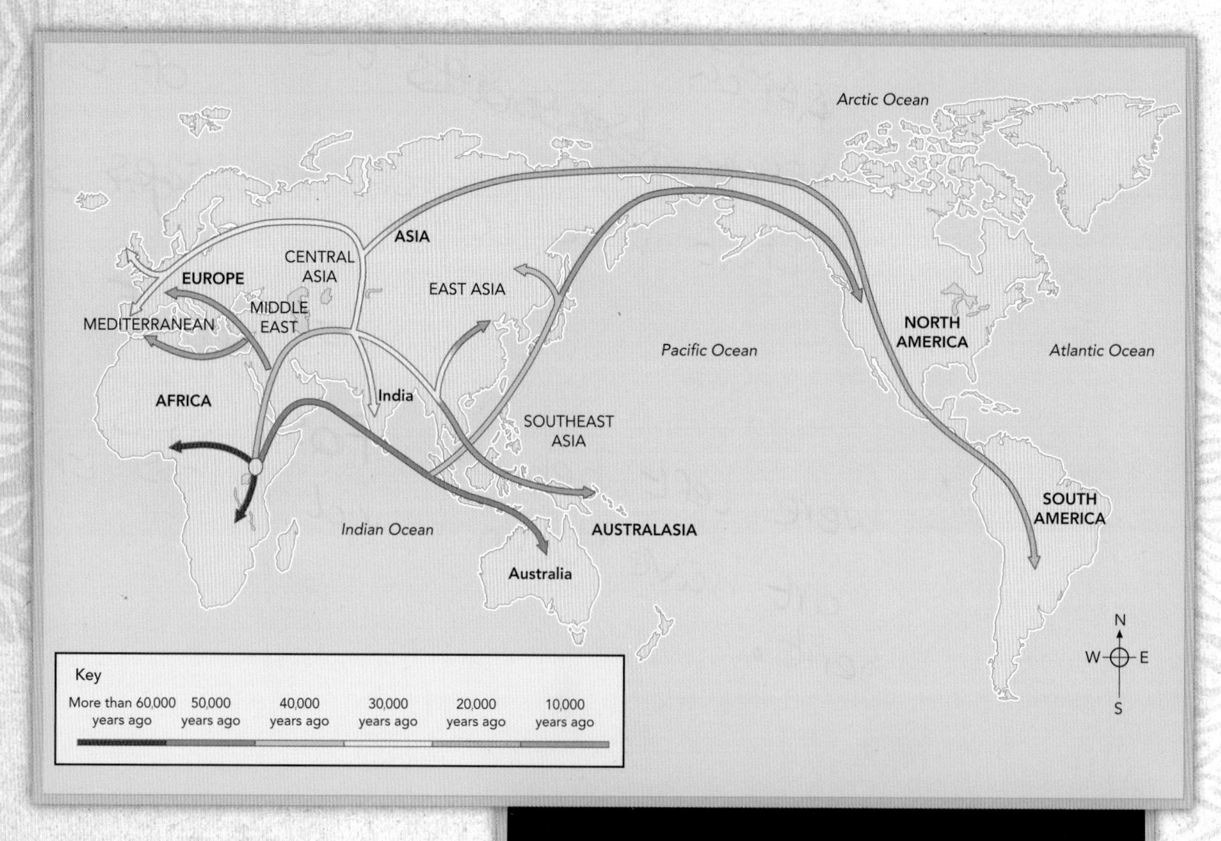


This map shows how humankind first spread across the world from Africa.

## Twenty-first century science

Every human has a unique biological code that makes them slightly different from all other humans. We call this code **DNA**. Scientists have used DNA as another way to discover the starting point of humankind. This is made possible because parts of our DNA are only passed from mothers to their children. Scientists can follow these parts back for thousands of years. In this way they have shown that modern humans all came from the same original DNA around 171,500 years ago. This is about the time that the first modern humans were thought to be living in Africa.

Mary Leakey (left) carefully removes a fossil from a cliff at Olduvai Gorge, Tanzania, in 1965.

## The Leakey family

Mary and Louis Leakey made important discoveries of ancient human life in East Africa. In 1959 they found ancient remains in Olduvai Gorge in Tanzania. These helped scientists to work out when modern humans first appeared. Mary also found fossilized footprints that showed how our ancestors learned to walk about 3.5 million years ago. Their son Richard and his wife Meave have continued this work. In 1967 Richard found more ancient remains at Koobi Fora in northern Kenya. Meave and now their daughter Louise Leakey are still exploring the Koobi Fora region today.

## Getting brainier

As our ancestors **evolved** into modern humans, they became more intelligent. At the same time, their brains got bigger. Scientists believe this is a direct link – the bigger the brain, the cleverer they were! One way to see how intelligent people were millions of years ago is to look at the design of the tools they were using. For example, simple tools, such as sticks used for digging, developed into shaped tools, such as small axes or picks. Stone was used instead of wood. Sharpened stone flakes acted as early knives to cut meat.

## Hunter gatherers

Early humans lived by hunting and gathering. Animal bones and seeds that show this way of life have been found alongside ancient human remains. Weapons such as spears would have been used for hunting, and knives were used for preparing meat. **Charcoal** found near some remains shows that humans also used fire a very long time ago.

This ancient rock painting was found in the southern Sahara Desert, Libya. It shows hunters carrying bows and arrows.

## Bambuti pygmies

The Bambuti have lived in the **rainforest** of Congo DR for at least 4,500 years. Their lives are similar to those of our ancient human ancestors. They get their food by hunting, fishing, and gathering using nets, spears, and small bows and arrows. Their homes are small beehive-shaped huts made from a frame of sticks and filled in with leaves. These are temporary shelters as the Bambuti move to a new part of the forest each month. They get everything they need from the rainforest. The Bambuti do not have chiefs or leaders. Problems or arguments are solved by general discussion.

The Bambuti are pygmies, which means they are shorter than the average human. On average they grow no taller than 137 centimetres (4 feet 6 inches) in height.

This Bambuti pygmy is a hunter gatherer from the village of Ntandi in Uganda.

# Early civilization

Africa was home to one of the world's most famous ancient **civilizations**. The Ancient Egyptians were ruled by powerful Egyptian kings called **pharaohs** and were a highly developed society. They lived around the floodplains of the River Nile between around 3000 BCE and 670 BCE. The floodplains provided the Ancient Egyptians with **fertile** soils and easy access to water. They developed new technology that allowed them to use the water for growing **crops**. This is known as **irrigation** and was not used by other human societies until much later.

## Daily life

Most Ancient Egyptians were farmers. They lived in small mud huts and grew cereal crops such as barley and wheat, as well as some vegetables and fruits. The fertile soils meant that they produced more than enough food to meet their own needs. The rest would be given to the pharaoh as a form of **tax** and gathered into huge stores. Fishing and hunting were another way that people got food. Many birds **migrated** along the Nile and could be trapped. Deer were also hunted, though normally only by the rich.

## Kings of Egypt

Egyptian kings, or pharaohs, had absolute rule over their land and people. The best officers would help the pharaoh to control the kingdom. They would collect produce from farmers for storage and organize projects such as building irrigation channels. Food was given out in return for work or during times of shortages. Pharaohs were greatly respected and treated as a god on Earth, alongside Ra, the god of the sun, and Osiris, the god of the dead.

This wall painting from around 1500 BCE shows scenes from the different farming seasons of Ancient Egypt – one of the world's earliest civilizations.

## Africa Fact

Death was of great importance to the Ancient Egyptians. They believed it was part of a journey to the next life. Many people would keep treasured items to be buried with them for this journey.

Ancient Egyptian farmers used animals to help them do the hard work in the fields.

## Expert builders

The Ancient Egyptians were talented builders. Their skill can be seen in the pyramids at Giza, near Cairo, which show great knowledge of mathematics and **engineering**. A huge system of organized labour was needed to build them, with thousands of men moving large blocks of stone across the desert. The pyramids were built as royal burial chambers, but were raided by thieves who stole the pharaohs' treasures. Later, Egyptian pharaohs were buried in the "Valley of the Kings". Their **tombs** were dug deep into the surrounding mountains and covered with earth to hide and protect them from thieves.

## The secrets of Ancient Egypt

In 1922, the tomb of a young pharaoh called Tutankhamen was found. It was located in the Valley of the Kings and had been untouched for almost 3,000 years! The treasures inside included a **chariot**, furniture, weapons, and many jewels. Tutankhamen was only about 18 years old when he died. His body was found inside three coffins, two of wood and one of solid gold!

## Mummification

**Mummification** was a process to **preserve** human bodies for their journey into the next life. Only the wealthiest could afford to have their bodies mummified. First, the internal organs such as the lungs, liver, and stomach (but not the heart) were removed and dried out using a salt called natron. The brain was also removed by smashing it with a hook and pulling it through the nose! The empty body was then covered in natron to dry it out for around 40 days. Once dry, the body was washed and the dried organs put back in. Sawdust or other dry material was used to stuff the body, and oils made the skin look soft and more lifelike again. The body was then carefully wrapped in many layers of linen before being placed in a coffin ready for burial.

This small solid-gold coffin is one of four containers from the tomb of Tutankhamen. The pharaoh's internal organs were placed in them as part of the process of mummification.

## Hieroglyphics

Events and stories in Ancient Egypt were recorded using a system known as **hieroglyphics**. This is where symbols and pictures, called hieroglyphs, are used instead of letters.

The meaning of hieroglyphics remained something of a mystery until 1799, when a black stone with carved writing on it was found at Rosetta in northern Egypt. Known as the Rosetta Stone, the writing on it recorded events from around 200 BCE in Egyptian and Greek. By comparing the Egyptian hieroglyphs with the Greek alphabet, experts managed to work out what hieroglyphics meant for the first time.

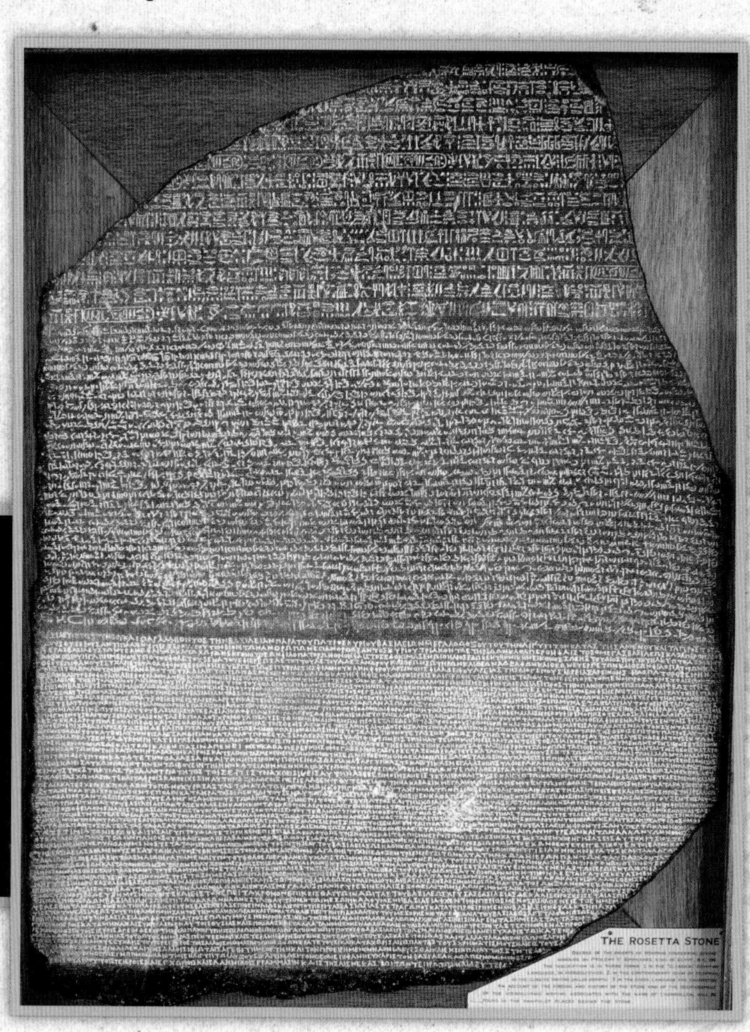


The Rosetta Stone helped experts to unravel the mystery of hieroglyphics and understand more about life in Ancient Egypt.

## The Kushites and the Egyptians

The lands to the south of Ancient Egypt were known as Nubia and were home to another ancient civilization called the Kushites. They lived alongside the Ancient Egyptians from around 3000 BCE. They **traded** gold and other precious **minerals** with the Ancient Egyptians in return for grain. From around 2000 BCE, Nubia was directly controlled by the Ancient Egyptians and the Kushites adopted many Egyptian ways of living. They worshipped Egyptian gods and used pyramids to bury the dead, for example.

By around 800 BCE, Ancient Egypt had weakened and Kushite leaders began to conquer parts of Egypt. By 715 BCE they had taken control of all of Egypt, but only ruled for a short time. They were driven out in around 662 BCE by the Assyrians, another ancient civilization from Mesopotamia (part of modern-day Iraq and Turkey). The Kushite civilization returned to Nubia where it survived for a further 900 years. Its main city was at Meroë. During this time, the Nubians developed their own unique **culture**. For example, their system of writing changed from Egyptian hieroglyphics to a new Meroitic alphabet. Eventually, the Kushites were defeated following invasions from neighbouring Ethiopia.

The pyramids of Meroë were built as royal burial tombs. Today, they are Sudan's most popular tourist attraction.

# Great kingdoms

Africa has had many great kingdoms, where a king or leader has controlled an entire region and its people. From 1000 BCE until the late 1700s, these kingdoms were important centres of **trade**, craftsmanship, and learning.

## Ancient Ghana (around 300–1100 CE)

Ancient Ghana was in what is now Senegal and Mauritania. The people of the Ghana kingdom were the Soninke. They were brought together by a leader called Dinga Cisse. The **empire** gained wealth by mining and trading in gold. They used camels to transport gold across the Sahara Desert to the Middle East.

The 11th-century geographer Al-Bakri described Ancient Ghana as having the richest gold mines in the world. He wrote:

"The King ... puts on a high cap decorated with gold and wrapped in a **turban** of fine cotton. He holds an audience in a domed pavilion around which stand ten horses covered with gold-embroidered materials and on his right, are the sons of the ... kings of his country, wearing splendid clothes and their hair plaited with gold."

### AFRICA FACT

One thing that Ancient Ghana traded for gold was salt. But the salt traders and Ghanaians did not understand each other. To solve this, it is said they used a system of "silent trade". Salt traders would leave salt at an agreed place for the Ghanaian traders to inspect. The Ghanaians would then leave an amount of gold that they were willing to pay. When the salt traders returned, they would count the gold. If they were happy then they would leave and the Ghanaians would collect their salt. If they were unhappy then they would leave again until the Ghanaians left more gold. This unusual silent trade would have needed a great deal of trust!

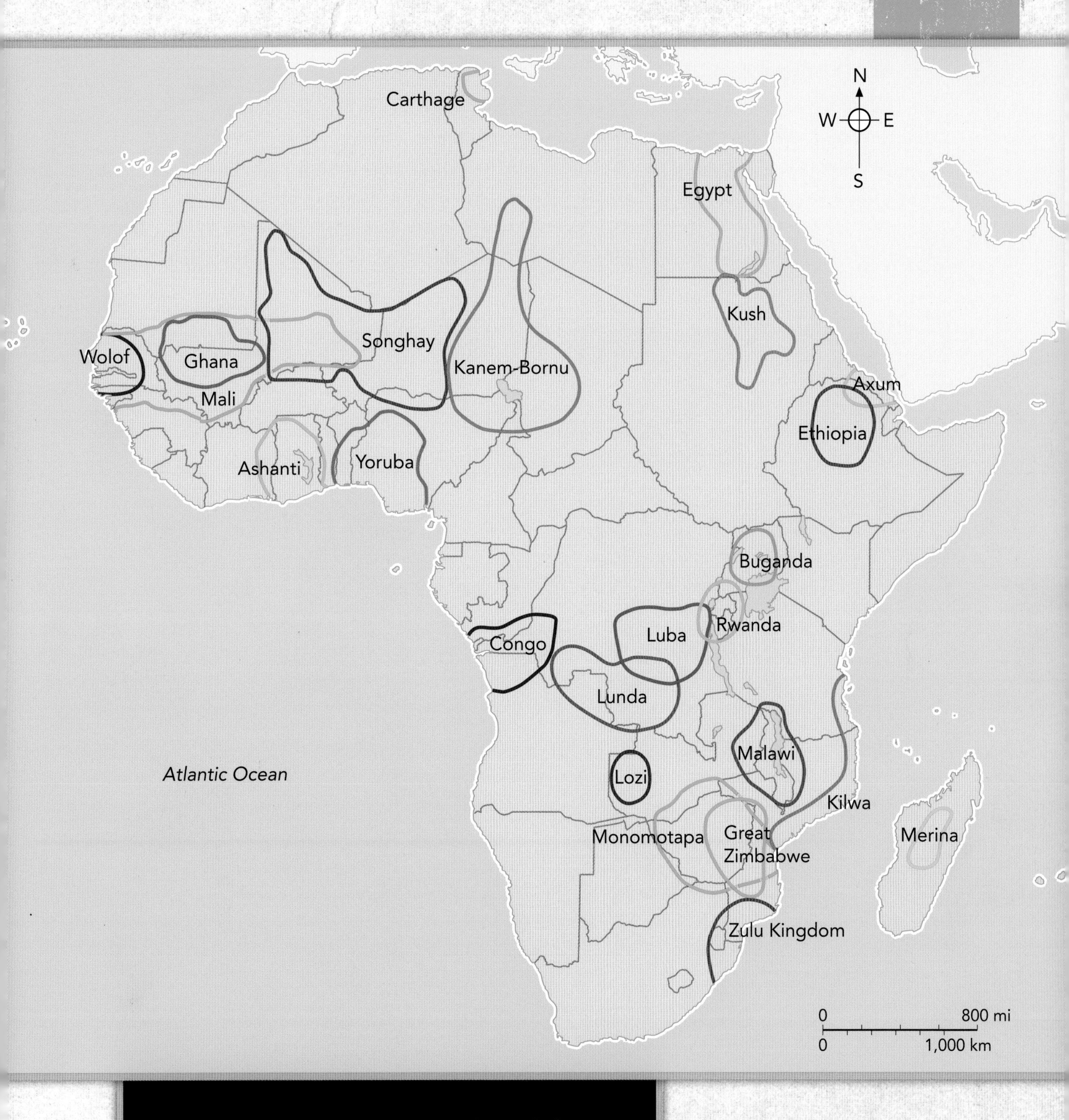


This map shows the location and spread of some of Africa's best known early kingdoms or societies. The coloured lines show where the boundaries used to be.

## Mali Empire

The Mali Empire was created by a **warrior** called Sundiata. He brought together the **clans** and rulers of West Africa as a single empire in around 1235 CE. Within 100 years the Mali Empire controlled trade in the whole region and stretched around 2,000 kilometres (1,250 miles) across West Africa. As well as trade, the Mali Empire created important centres of learning and religion. Many important **mosques** were built during this time, including the Great Mosque at Djenne – the largest mud-brick building in the world.

The Great Mosque at Djenne was built around the 1200s but was later destroyed. This new version of the mosque was built in the early 1900s.

## Mansa Musa

Mansa Musa ruled the Mali Empire from 1312–1337. He was well known for his extravagant spending! In 1324 he made a famous **pilgrimage** to Mecca in Saudi Arabia, the holiest place in Islam. He took over 60,000 people with him, including at least 12,000 **slaves**. He used his wealth to buy luxury goods wherever he went and gave expensive gifts to rulers he met along the way.

## Islam and learning

By the time of the Mali Empire, Islam had become the main religion of North and West Africa. It had arrived with traders from the Middle East. The same traders also introduced new ideas and knowledge which they shared with local scholars. Cities such as Timbuktu in Mali soon became important centres of learning as well as trade. By the mid-14th century, Timbuktu had three universities with over 25,000 students. These included Sankore University, one of the oldest in the world, which was partly built under the orders of Mansa Musa.

## Africa Fact

From the 1300s to the 1500s, Sankore University had more foreign students than New York University does today.

## Great Zimbabwe (1100–1500 CE)

Great Zimbabwe was a city and major centre of trade in southern Africa. Gold, **ivory**, beads, cloth, and **porcelain** were among the goods traded with countries as far away as China. At its height, around 18,000 people lived in Great Zimbabwe. At the centre of the city was the Great Enclosure, which had thick walls similar to European castles. The ruins of Great Zimbabwe can still be seen in modern Zimbabwe today, and gave the country its name.

This is the Great Enclosure in Great Zimbabwe. It is the largest of the many stone built structures, and is a reminder of the important kingdom that once thrived there.

## Kongo (around 1390–1914 CE)

Kongo was one of the largest ancient kingdoms in Central Africa. It was led by a king known as "Manikongo". The Kongo formed close links with Portugal after the Portuguese arrived in the region in 1483. These links were so strong that Manikongo and his son were even **baptized** and given the Christian names João and Afonso.

Portuguese settlers were at first welcomed in Kongo, but their role in the Atlantic slave trade (see page 36) meant that the relationship became less friendly. After internal fighting weakened the Kongo, it became part of the Portuguese **colony** of Angola in 1914.

## A language kingdom

Swahili is a language that developed through trade between African and Arab people along the coastline of East Africa. African ivory and gold were exchanged for cloth and spices from the east. As the traders mixed, Arabic words became combined with local Bantu languages. Swahili emerged as a new language. The language gets its name from the Arabic *sawahili*, which means "of the coast".

### Some Swahili words

Below are a few common Swahili words that you might have heard of:

*jambo* – hello
*safari* – journey
*asante* – thanks
*bwana* – sir
*simba* – lion
*hakuna matata* – no problem.

# Daily life

Much of what we know about Ancient Africa comes from the stories of travellers such as Leo Africanus. For some **cultures**, such as the Ancient Egyptians or Great Zimbabweans, there are physical remains that also give us clues. Another important type of knowledge is oral history. This is the spoken knowledge that is passed down from one generation to the next. It can teach us a lot about day to day life in the past.

## Leo Africanus

Leo Africanus was a Spanish Moroccan writer and traveller. Here he describes Timbuktu, in West Africa, around 1510 CE.

"The houses there are very poor, except for those of the king and his nobles. The **merchants** are exceedingly rich and large numbers of black Africans continually come here to buy cloth brought from Barbarie (Morocco) and Europe ..."

## The riches of power

Power in Ancient Africa was often shown by the wealth of its rulers. There are stories of palaces and royal rooms decorated in gold and silk and overflowing with food. Besides the ruler and their protectors and advisors, the court would often include important merchants, scholars, and religious leaders. **Trade** was an important source of wealth, but many rulers also collected **taxes** from their people. These were often paid in the form of crops or cattle rather than as money.

## African slavery

Slavery dates back to the Ancient Egyptians and was an important trade for many early African kingdoms. Working as a **slave** on the land or in the home of a master was part of everyday life for hundreds of thousands of people. In the Kanem kingdom of West Africa, up to a third of all people were enslaved. Similar numbers of slaves were found in the kingdoms of Ghana, Mali, and Songhay.

Tribal leaders may not hold much political control in Africa today, but they are still culturally important. This is a Nigerian tribal leader dressed in traditional clothing at a gathering of tribal peoples in Nigeria.

## A working life

Most people in Ancient Africa spent their days working on the land. They used basic tools, such as an *adze*, or **hoe**, and grew crops to feed their families. In coastal areas and near major rivers, fishing was an important activity. In drier parts of Africa, people kept **livestock** instead of growing **crops**. They would often move with their animals to find water or fresh **pasture**.

Hunting and gathering was another activity for several ancient societies. If people needed things, they would trade their own crops, fish, or livestock for other goods. Markets became important places for people to meet and exchange these products. Markets are still important across Africa today, though goods are mainly bought and sold for money now, rather than exchanged.

## Staple diets

The main (staple) food eaten by different communities in Ancient Africa was linked to what they could grow or trade for in their local area. Different parts of the **continent** had different specialities. Many of these are still the main staple foods today.

| Food type | Description | Where it is found |
|---|---|---|
| Couscous | Made from semolina flour (from wheat) and eaten with meat, vegetables, fish, and spicy sauces. | Morocco, Algeria, Tunisia, and other parts of northern Africa. |
| Yams | A root vegetable that can be boiled, fried, or pounded to make a type of porridge called “fufu”. | Across West and Central Africa, but especially popular in Nigeria and Ghana. |
| Maize | A cereal crop that is roasted (as cobs) or dried and ground into a flour for making porridge or bread. | Throughout sub-Saharan Africa, and a staple food in southern and eastern Africa. |

In parts of rural Africa many people still live in family compounds. The women from this village, in Burkina Faso, are famous for painting their compounds with colourful motifs.

## Bark cloth

Clothing in Ancient Africa was normally made from simple cloth or animal skins. A more unusual fabric used for clothing was bark cloth. In Uganda this was made from the bark of a fig tree. The bark was first stripped and soaked in water to soften it. It could then be hammered flat to make a fabric. In Uganda bark cloth was especially worn by royalty and chiefs during official ceremonies. It was also used to wrap the dead before they were buried. An important chief may be wrapped in up to 200 pieces! Bark cloth is still used in parts of Uganda today.

## Skills and crafts

As farming became more organized in early African societies, some people were freed from working the land and developed new skills and crafts. Many of these were linked to materials available in the local area. This gave particular **ethnic groups** a reputation for certain skills or crafts. The Akamba people in Kenya, for example, are well known for their skill in drum making. In southern Africa, the Zulu and Ndebele people are famous for their beautiful bead work.

## Working with metal

The Nok Culture (500–200 BCE) in Nigeria was one of the earliest known societies to develop skills in ironwork. They used a furnace (oven) to heat up iron ore (rocks containing iron) in order to separate the iron from the rock. The iron could then be shaped into tools for farming, eating, and other uses.

Other ancient societies, such as Great Zimbabwe, also used iron for making tools and weapons. Metal working was also used to make jewellery and for art. The treasures of Tutankhamen are one of the most famous examples of this. They show that the Ancient Egyptians had developed great skill at working with gold. Another culture that showed great artistic skill was the Benin kingdom of West Africa. It is especially well known for its life-like bronze heads and sculptures, which are often known simply as "Benin bronzes".

This Benin bronze shows the face of a lion and is decorated with flowers.

You will find many examples of these colourful ceramic pots in markets across Africa today.

## Ceramics

Clay is found in many parts of Africa. It has been fired (heated) to make **ceramic** pots and other items since at least 500 BCE. Many ceramic items were made for use in cooking, or for storing and carrying goods such as water or milk. Over time, people developed the skills to make more shaped pieces and to decorate them with textures or paints.

# Trade and inventions

The Ancient Egyptians brought many inventions into the world. They developed digging sticks and **hoes** into an early type of **plough**, for example. Different types of **irrigation** technology were among their most important inventions.

One method of irrigation involved trapping water from the annual flooding of the Nile in specially-dug canals. A mechanism called a *shaduf* was then used to water the fields. A *shaduf* works like a pair of scales with a bucket on one end and a heavy weight on the other. The heavy weight helped to lift the filled bucket so that the water could then be tipped into a channel that took it to the fields.

## Building techniques

Buildings in Ancient Africa were often quite simple structures. They were made using locally available materials such as mud, sticks, and leaves, and varied in style from region to region. Most people had some skills in these simple building techniques.

Larger and more impressive buildings were normally built for kings and leaders, or as religious buildings. The pyramids, Great Zimbabwe, and the early **mosques** in West Africa are examples of this. How the Egyptians built such enormous and mathematically-exact structures as the pyramids, however, is still not known for certain.

## Lalibela and the rock-cut churches

Ethiopia is home to some of Ancient Africa's most unusual buildings. These are the rock-cut churches in the city of Lalibela. There are 11 churches in total, and they are cut out of solid granite in the ground. They show great skill and craftsmanship, and are thought to have been built by skilled Ethiopian **stonemasons**. Four of these churches – the House of Emmanuel, the House of Mercurios, Abba Libanos, and the House of Gabriel – are carved from one, single piece of rock.

Saint George's Church, in Lalibela, was one of the last rock-cut churches to be built, around 1250 CE. It is carved from rock in the shape of a cross.

## Merchants and sellers

**Trade** has always been part of African life. Much of this was local, but some reached as far away as China. Early kingdoms, such as the Kanem **Empire**, grew strong by controlling trade routes in Africa. The Kanem controlled a large region of West Africa between the 9th and 19th centuries. They became wealthy by demanding payments from traders for safe access through their lands.

Salt was one of the main goods carried by camels. This camel caravan is crossing the salt flats at Lake Assal in Djibouti.

## Camel caravans

The trade routes crossing the Sahara Desert and on to Europe or Asia were some of the most important of the ancient world. One of the main ways to transport goods along these routes was by camel. Camels can live for days without food or water, and are used to the hot, dry desert conditions. Trade with camels normally involved large groups travelling together. These were known as camel caravans, and could have up to 20,000 camels!

## Africa Fact

The giving of gifts was an important part of trade relations for the Kanem-Bornu Empire. On one occasion the king presented the gift of a giraffe to the Sultan of Tunis!

## East African trade

Coins found in Zanzibar and Tanzania show that from around 300 CE, East Africa had strong trade links with North Africa, Persia, and India. This trade by sea was closely linked to seasonal winds that blew across the Indian Ocean. Between November and March the winds blew from the east, bringing **merchants** with cloth, spices, and sugar. The merchants would trade their goods for **ivory**, gold, and **slaves**. They would then make their return journey when the winds changed and blew from the west, between April and October.

These traditional sailing boats are known as *dhow* along the coast of East Africa and *felucca* in Egypt.

# Invasion and exploration

By the 1400s European explorers had heard stories of Africa's great riches, and were becoming interested in exploring the land for their own gain. Africa was also on the European ocean routes to Asia. Stopping on Africa's coast provided a chance to rest and to take on supplies or new **trade**. Over time, Europeans established trading posts on Africa's coast where their ships could habour in safety and store or transfer goods. Contact with Africa made others curious to explore inland from the coast. This led to an age of European exploration that brought Europeans into contact with the **cultures** of Ancient Africa. This was to change Africa forever, and in many ways marked the end of Ancient Africa.

Mungo Park (1771-1806) was a Scottish explorer and one of the first Europeans to travel in West Africa. This sketch shows him coming across a lion.

## European settlements

The first Europeans to settle in Africa were the Portuguese and Dutch. The Portuguese had small coastal settlements in what are now Angola and Mozambique. The Dutch settled in South Africa in 1652, where they founded what is now the city of Cape Town. The first settlers were farmers and became known as boers, which means farmer in the Dutch language. They provided food for ships on their way to India. Later, the Dutch settlers called themselves *Afrikaners* ("Africans") and this term is still used by their descendants today.

## Cetshwayo, the Zulu warrior

Cetshwayo was a Zulu **warrior** who defeated the British army when they tried to take control of Zululand in January 1879. In July 1879 the British returned and this time captured Zululand from Cetshwayo. In 1882 Cetshwayo travelled to London to ask Queen Victoria for the return of his Zulu kingdom. He was granted his wish, but his powers as king were greatly reduced. When he returned, Zululand was in civil war. Cetshwayo himself died in 1884, marking the end of the Zulu kingdom.

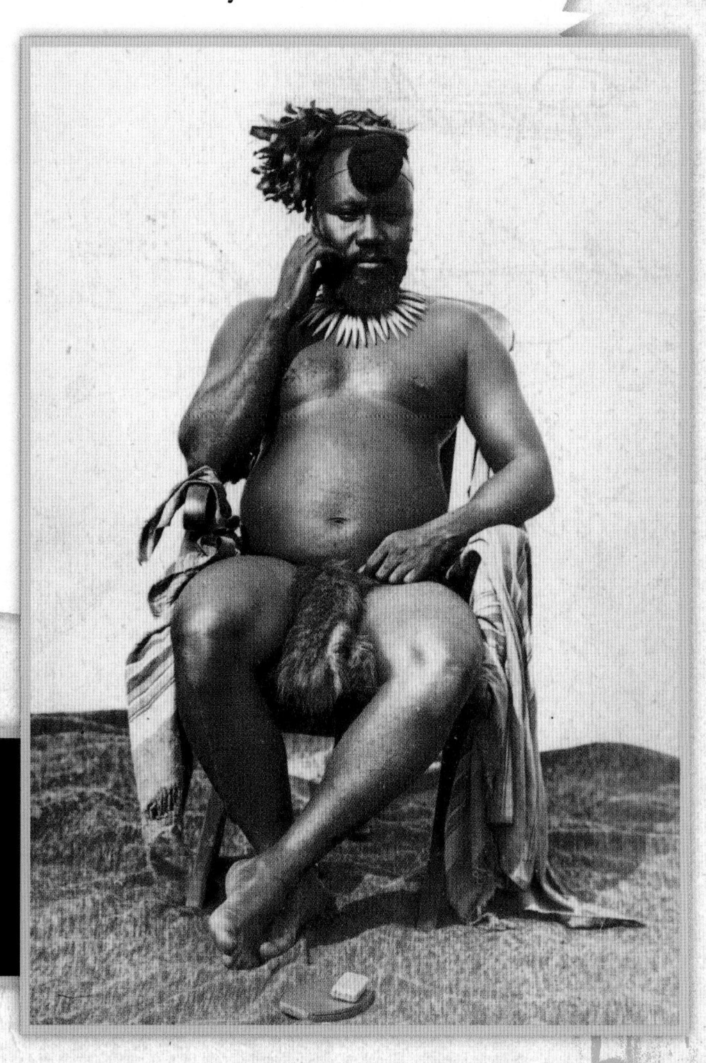

This photograph of Cetshwayo, the Zulu warrior, was taken in 1880.

## The beginnings of the slave trade

Slavery had been part of African life for centuries. **Slaves** were traded by many of the early kingdoms.

## East African slavery

By the 1700s, slavery was a major trade on the East African coast, with slaves sold to work in the Middle East and Asia. Brazilian traders also took slaves from East Africa, and the French bought slaves for their sugar and coffee **plantations** on the islands of Mauritius and Réunion. This early trade in slaves was controlled by Arabs and Africans. Zanzibar and Mombasa became major centres for the slave trade.

## Slave traders

African slave traders would travel with small private armies and raid villages to capture people to sell as slaves. Sometimes these slave traders were working for African rulers. Tippu Tip, for example, was a famous slave trader who worked for the Sultans of Zanzibar. Other slave traders were private businessmen who became very wealthy.

Once they were captured, slaves would normally be chained together using metal chains or ropes. These were attached to wooden boards around the necks of the slaves. The slave trade took place in markets, like other trades. Some slaves would not survive the journey to market and others were so weak by the time they got there, that they fetched only a very low price.

### Tippu Tip (1837–1905)

Tippu Tip, or Muhammed Bin Hamid, was born on the island of Zanzibar to an Arab mother and African father. He built a trading empire on the African mainland, dealing mainly in ivory and slaves. His men controlled an area that stretched over 1,000 kilometres (620 miles) inland from the coast of Tanzania. Tippu Tip also owned large plantations on Zanzibar that grew cloves – a valuable spice that is still grown there today.

Tippu Tip had around 10,000 slaves working for him on his plantations.

# Slavery and colonialism

In the mid-1400s, the **slave trade** in West Africa began to be controlled by European traders.

The Portuguese began to take slaves to work in their new **colonies** in South America. Then, in 1518, the Spanish began to transport slaves to their new colonies in the Caribbean Islands. Soon the French, British, and Dutch also became involved. Each nation used different trading posts along the West African coast to buy slaves and ship them to the Americas. There they would be sold to work on European-owned **plantations** growing sugar, cotton, tobacco, coffee, and other **crops**. These were then shipped back to Europe on the empty slave ships.

The transatlantic slave trade had a major impact on the population of Africa. By the mid-19th century, at least 12 million Africans had been captured and transported as slaves. Most ended up on the islands of the Caribbean or in Brazil. Around five per cent were sold into slavery in North America, mostly into what are now the southern states of the USA. Slaves were treated as less human than their white slave owners and lived in miserable conditions.

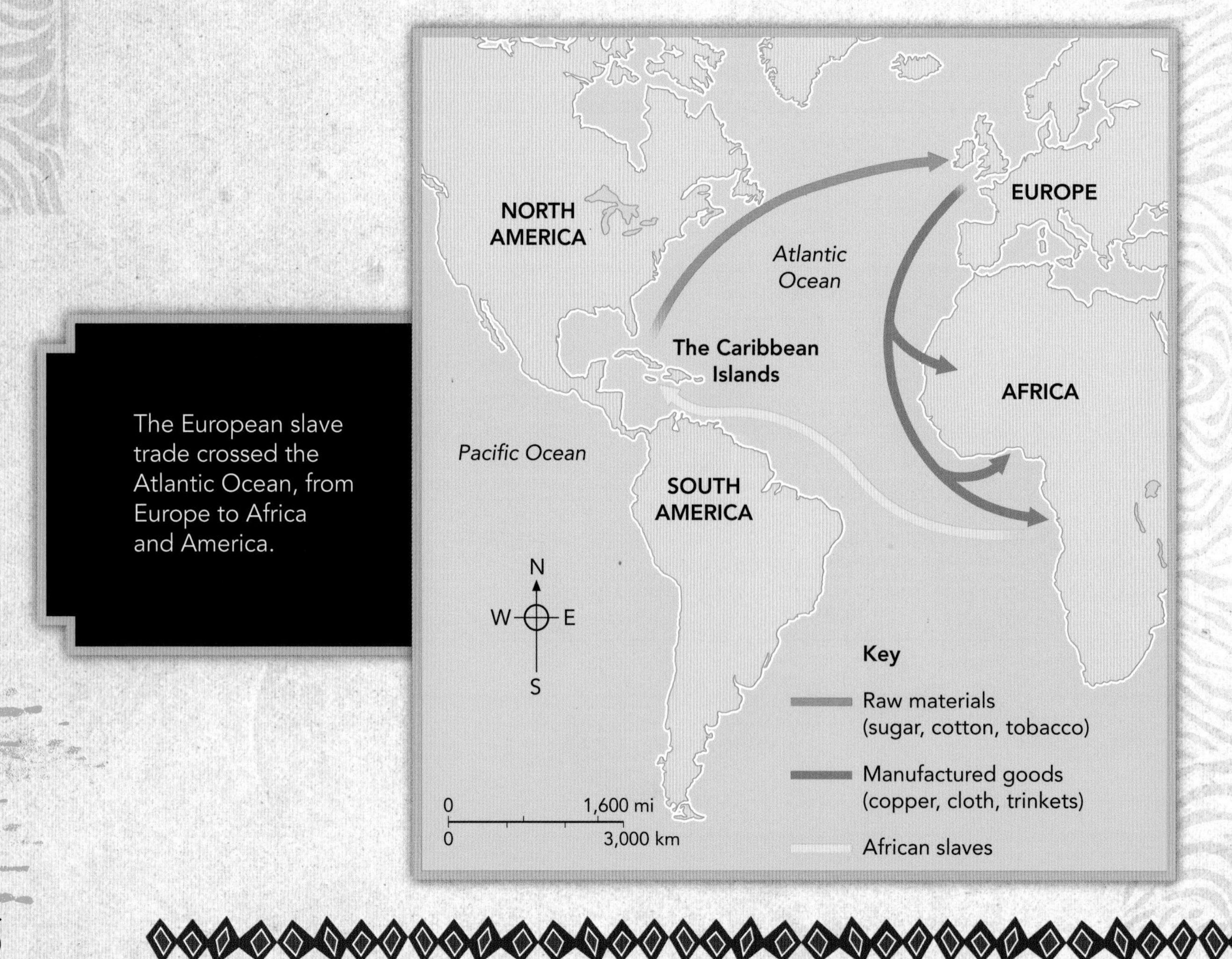


The European slave trade crossed the Atlantic Ocean, from Europe to Africa and America.

## Surviving the Middle Passage

The Middle Passage was the name given to the 6,500 kilometre (4,000 mile) journey from Africa to the Americas. This could take up to 3 months and slaves lived in terrible conditions. Up to 20 per cent of them died on the journey.

The former slave Olaudah Equiano spoke about the conditions on his journey. He said:

"I became so sick … I was not able to eat, nor had I the least desire to taste anything. I now wished for … death, to relieve me; but soon, to my grief, two of the white men offered me eatables; and on my refusing to eat, one of them … laid me across I think the windlass, and tied my feet, while the other whipped me severely."

Olaudah Equiano was a former slave. He earned enough money to buy his freedom, and spent the next 20 years travelling the world.

## The end of slavery

Not everyone in Europe was in favour of the slave trade. By the late-1700s a campaign to end slavery had begun in Britain, led by **abolitionists** such as William Wilberforce. There were several reasons for this. Machines had been invented that could work more efficiently than slaves. Britain had also lost its American colonies during the American War of Independence in 1776. This meant it no longer directly benefited from the slave plantations in the Americas.

In 1807 the British government banned slave trading, and from 1834 it became **illegal** to own slaves. Other European nations were slower to give up slavery, and slavery in Europe did not finally end until the early part of the 1900s. In the United States, slavery became illegal in 1865.

Many former slaves continued to live hard lives after slavery ended. These people are picking cotton on an American plantation in 1895.

This image shows members of the Liberian government in 1893. The government was mostly made up of freed African American slaves who returned to Liberia when it was given its freedom.

## Early African colony

Sierra Leone is a country that was created by the end of slavery. It began to receive freed slaves from former British colonies in the Americas in 1792. The former slaves settled in an area that became called Freetown. Freetown is still the capital of Sierra Leone today – a permanent reminder of the origins of the country. In 1808 Freetown was made a colony of the British Empire, one of the first European colonies in Africa.

## A weakened land

Four hundred years of slavery had greatly weakened African societies. Kingdoms that had once been strong became weak and vulnerable. There was an increase in fighting between communities that had once lived happily together and this further weakened them. This meant that when the Europeans arrived to **colonize** parts of Africa, many societies were simply too weak to resist them.

## The Scramble for Africa

At first, Europeans had little interest in governing Africa. They were more interested in trading goods such as **ivory**, spices, gold, and slaves. As more countries became interested in this trade, however, nations began to protect their trade by taking control of parts of the **continent**. The discovery of valuable **resources**, such as gold and diamonds in South Africa and copper in Zambia, made these pressures even greater. Soon, European nations were desperately competing to control as much of the continent as possible. This became known as the Scramble for Africa. Little attention was paid by the European powers to the interests of African people.

## Berlin Conference

In 1884, the 14 countries that already had interests in Africa were invited to a special conference in Berlin. The meeting was to agree trade rules and colonial boundaries in Africa. Not a single African was at the meeting! By the end of the conference, Africa had been divided into 50 new colonies. The boundaries of these colonies were drawn with no thought for existing African societies. Some were simply straight lines on a map that divided entire **cultures**.

This cartoon about the Berlin Conference of 1884 shows the European leaders "cutting up" Africa as if it were a large cake.

The Englishman Cecil Rhodes was one of the most famous of Africa's colonists. He was Prime Minister of the Cape Colony in South Africa, and began the De Beers diamond-mining company, which is still famous today.

## Changed forever

European colonialism in Africa lasted in most parts of the continent for less than 100 years, but changed many countries enormously. New languages and religions were introduced. Land was taken and local cultures were destroyed. But despite all these changes and the effects that continue today, it is important to remember that Africa has its own pre-colonial history – a history that is richer and older than almost any other on Earth.

# Timeline

| | |
|---|---|
| **3.5 million years ago** | Very early **ancestors** begin to walk in the upright position. |
| **1.6 million years ago** | The human ancestor *Homo habilis* is living in Africa. |
| **170,000 BCE** | *Homo sapiens* evolve in East Africa, spreading throughout the **continent** and globe. |
| **3000 BCE –670 BCE** | Ancient Egyptians live around the floodplains of the Nile Delta. |
| **715 BCE** | Kushites from neighbouring Nubia conquer Egypt and rule until 662 BCE. |
| **500–200 BCE** | Nok society smelt iron in furnaces to create tools. |
| **300–1100 CE** | Kingdom of Ancient Ghana is an important centre of **trade**, craftsmanship, and learning. |
| **1100–1500** | Great Zimbabwe is a city and major centre of trade in southern Africa. |
| **1235** | Mali Empire begins to spread across West Africa under the rule of Sundiata. |
| **1324** | Mansa Musa, a ruler of the Mali Empire, makes a pilgrimage to Mecca in Saudi Arabia, taking 60,000. |
| **1390–1914** | The Kongo kingdom is strong, and has links with Portugal for many years. |

**1652** Dutch settlers found the city of Cape Town in what is now South Africa.

**1799** The Rosetta Stone is found, with writings in Egyptian **hieroglyphics** and Greek, allowing experts to begin decoding and understanding Egyptian writings.

**1795** The British land at the Cape of Good Hope.

**1807–1860** The Transatlantic **slave** trade ends, after 400 years of slavery, and around 12 million people being shipped from Africa to the Americas.

**1865** Slavery ends in the United States of America at the end of the American Civil War.

**1879** The British-Zulu War is fought between the British Empire and the Zulu Empire.

**1884** European nations meet at the Berlin Conference to divide Africa into **colonies**, and agree trade rules concerning the continent.

**1922** The Ancient Egyptian **tomb** of Tutankhamen is discovered in the Valley of the Kings

**1959** Mary and Louis Leakey find ancient remains in Olduvai Gorge, Tanzania.

**1990–2003** US Human Genome Project uses DNA research to find out more about (among other things) the origins of humans.

# Glossary

**abolitionist** person who supported the ending of slavery

**ancestor** family member who has died a long time ago

**baptize** to perform the ceremony of baptism, by which a person becomes a member of the Christian faith

**ceramic** object made of clay which has been hardened by being baked in an oven

**charcoal** fuel made from burned wood

**chariot** two-wheeled horse-drawn carriage used in battle

**civilization** society with a high level of art, science, and government

**clan** large group of families who are related to each other

**colonize** to make another country a colony of your own country

**colony** land controlled by another country

**continent** one of the main areas of land on Earth. Many countries may be found in one continent.

**crop** plant grown for use by people, such as cereals or vegetables

**culture** actions and beliefs of a society

**DNA** deoxyribonucleic acid; material found in each living cell that contains instructions on how that cell should behave and function

**empire** nation that is responsible for ruling several countries at once

**engineering** the application of scientific and mathematical knowledge in order to find solutions to practical problems such as building, construction, and mining

**ethnic group** people who share culture and language

**evolve** to develop certain qualities or characteristics through generations of offspring

**fertile** rich in materials or health needed for growth

**fossil** plant or animal whose remains have been preserved or have left a record in rock

**hieroglyphics** system of recording information using symbols and pictures known as hieroglyphs

**hoe** tool with a flat blade and a long handle used for planting, weeding, and gardening

**illegal** against the law

**irrigation** to bring water to crops and fields by digging ditches, laying pipes, or through other means

**ivory** material that comes from animal tusks, especially those of elephants

**livestock** animals kept for use or profit, such as farm animals

**merchant** person who buys and sells goods

**migrate** to move from one country or region and settle in another

**mineral** non-organic natural substances found in the earth

**mosque** place of worship for Muslims

**mummification** process by which a dead body is preserved by embalming, drying, and wrapping in cloth

**pasture** farmland which is used for feeding animals, such as cows and sheep, rather than growing crops

**pharaoh** Ancient Egyptian ruler

**pilgrimage** journey to a place of religious worship

**plantation** large farm on which crops are grown in large quantities by people who live and work there

**plough** to turn over soil in preparation for planting crops

**porcelain** fine, hard, thin ceramic

**preserve** to prevent from decaying

**primitive** basic; in an early stage of development

**rainforest** thick, forested area in a tropical region which supports a huge diversity of plant and animal life

**resource** mineral or raw material that is used in industry, business, and government to produce goods or services

**slave** person who is forced to work for another

**species** particular type of animal or plant

**stonemason** person who is skilled in using stone to make buildings

**tax** money that the government collects from people and businesses in order to finance the running of the country

**tomb** place where a person is buried

**trade** buy and sell goods

**turban** long piece of cloth wound round the head

**warrior** person engaged in a battle or fighting for a particular cause

# Find out more

## Books

*Continents in Close-up: Africa*, Malcolm Porter (Cherrytree Books, 2007)

*Continents of the World: Africa*, Rob Bowden (Hodder Wayland, 2007)

*Regions of the World: Africa South of the Sahara*, Rob Bowden (Heinemann Library, 2007)

*Regions of the World: The Middle East and North Africa*, Rob Bowden (Heinemann Library, 2007)

*The Ancient Egyptians (History Opens Windows)*, Jane Shuter (Heinemann Library, 2006)

## Websites

BBC World Service
**www.bbc.co.uk/worldservice/africa/features/storyofafrica**
This site explains the history of Africa and its people.

British Museum
**www.ancientegypt.co.uk**
Use this site to find out all you want to know about Ancient Egyptian people and their culture.

Kidipede
**www.historyforkids.org/learn/africa**
This website for children describes many different aspects of Ancient Africa.

## Places to visit

Many museums have good collections of African art and **culture**. Here are some examples:

**British Empire and Commonwealth Museum**
Clock Tower Yard
Temple Meads
Bristol
BS1 6QH
Tel: +44(0)117 925 4980
www.empiremuseum.co.uk

**The British Museum**
Great Russell Street
London
WC1B 3DG
Tel: +44 (0)20 7323 8299
www.britishmuseum.org

**World Museum Liverpool**
William Brown Street
Liverpool
L3 8EN
Tel: +44(0)151 478 4393
www.liverpoolmuseums.org.uk

# Index